MUSICIANS INSTITUTE TM

PRIVATE LESSONS

EXOTIC
Scales & Licks
for Guitar

by
Jean Marc Belkadi

16 TANTALIZING SCALES
&
80 GREAT WAYS TO USE THEM

Cover photo inserts by Peter Amft

ISBN 978-0-634-08475-1

HAL•LEONARD®
CORPORATION

7777 W. BLUEMOUND RD. P.O. BOX 13819 MILWAUKEE, WI 53213

In Australia Contact:
Hal Leonard Australia Pty. Ltd.
4 Lentara Court
Cheltenham, Victoria, 3192 Australia
Email: ausadmin@halleonard.com

Visit Hal Leonard Online at
www.halleonard.com

Introduction

The exotic scales in this book can be thought of as scales that are not related to the standard major or minor scales. Most of them have seven notes, but a few have more or less. They provide an excellent source for technical improvisation/composition and work in many styles, such as rock, jazz, funk, pop, and R&B.

This book contains a total of 80 examples (five for each exotic scale), and its purpose is to show you how to use these scales in any chord combination from the harmonized scale. Each exotic scale is harmonized with its respective chord on each scale degree, giving you a better understanding of the scale's sound and its possible harmonies.

The examples are recorded over grooves featuring a full rhythm section, so you'll have a good overview of how to use the scales in your own music. Each example is repeated at tempo a few times, after which it's played very slowly so you can hear each and every note. The licks don't progress in any particular order, so feel free to skip around to the ones you like. Enjoy.

Jean-Marc

Thanks to:

All at Hal Leonard Corporation
Ernesto Homeyer (for transcribing these examples)
Jon J. Hyman (sequencing and tracking)
Danny Osuma (for mastering the audio recording)
Beth Marlis, from Musicians Institute
Steve Blucher, from Dimarzio
Joseph Iacobellis, from Everly Strings (www.everlymusic.com)
Jude Gold, from Guitar Player

Table of Contents

	Page	CD Track
Prometheus Scale	4	1–5
Enigmatic Scale	6	6–10
Hebrew Scale (Ahavoh Rabboh)	8	11–15
Hungarian Gypsy Minor Scale	10	16–20
Hindu Scale	12	21–25
Neapolitan Major Scale	14	26–30
Neapolitan Minor Scale	16	31–35
East Indian Scale (Raga Todi)	18	36–40
Romanian Scale	20	41–45
Double Harmonic Minor Scale	22	46–50
Persian Scale	24	51–55
Double Augmented Scale	26	56–60
Eight-Tone Spanish Scale	28	61–65
Byzantine Scale	30	66–70
Overtone Scale	32	71–75
Harmonic Major Scale	34	76–80

Prometheus Scale

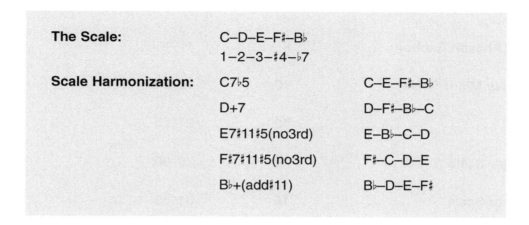

The Scale:	C–D–E–F♯–B♭	
	1–2–3–♯4–♭7	
Scale Harmonization:	C7♭5	C–E–F♯–B♭
	D+7	D–F♯–B♭–C
	E7♯11♯5(no3rd)	E–B♭–C–D
	F♯7♯11♯5(no3rd)	F♯–C–D–E
	B♭+(add♯11)	B♭–D–E–F♯

The first thing that comes to mind when looking at the harmonization of the Prometheus scale is the obvious relation to the whole tone scale, making it an excellent tool to use over altered V chords in major or minor, as well as static 7♯11 chords.

Example 1

This line uses the C Prometheus scale over a D pedal rock groove. Notice how closely this scale resembles the C whole tone scale; the only note missing is G♯.

Track 1

Example 2

Here's another C Prometheus line over an E pedal rock groove. The whole-tone quality makes sequencing an obvious choice, as demonstrated in this lick.

Track 2

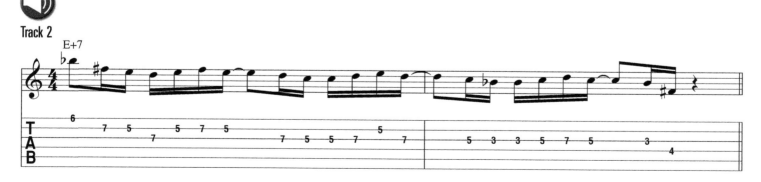

Example 3

This example exploits the tritone intervals from the Prometheus scale over an E pedal rock groove.

Track 3

Example 4

This example uses the C Prometheus scale over an E+7–D+7 progression.

Track 4

Example 5

Here's another example over the same E+7–D+7 progression.

Track 5

Enigmatic Scale

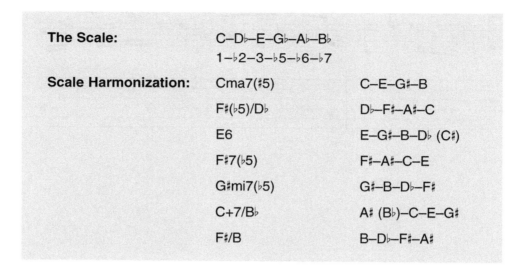

The Scale:	C–D♭–E–G♭–A♭–B♭	
	1–♭2–3–♭5–♭6–♭7	
Scale Harmonization:	Cma7(♯5)	C–E–G♯–B
	F♯(♭5)/D♭	D♭–F♯–A♯–C
	E6	E–G♯–B–D♭ (C♯)
	F♯7(♭5)	F♯–A♯–C–E
	G♯mi7(♭5)	G♯–B–D♭–F♯
	C+7/B♭	A♯ (B♭)–C–E–G♯
	F♯/B	B–D♭–F♯–A♯

Italian composer Giuseppe Verdi introduced the enigmatic scale in Western music. This scale can be seen as C altered (7th mode of D♭ melodic minor) without the ♯9 (E♭). It is very effective over an altered dominant chord.

Example 1

This is a sixteenth-note enigmatic scale lick over F♯7♭5. Practice it slowly first.

Track 6

Example 2

Here's a nice enigmatic eighth-note lick over F♯7♭5.

Track 7

Example 3

Here's a bi-tonal sweeping lick over F♯7♭5. This lick combines an F♯ major triad and a C augmented triad. All of the notes are included in the enigmatic scale.

Track 8

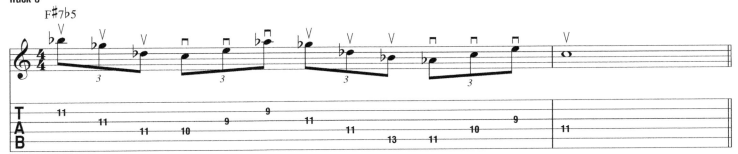

Example 4

Track 9

Here's another sixteenth-note enigmatic scale lick over F♯7♭5.

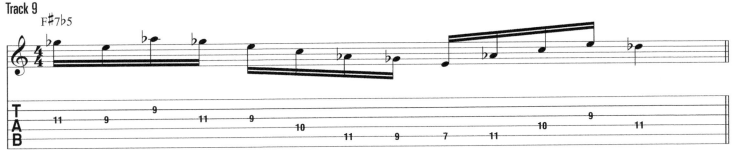

Example 5

Track 10

Here's another augmented sweeping idea with the enigmatic scale over F♯7♭5.

Hebrew Scale (Ahavoh Rabboh)

The Scale:	C–D♭–E–F–G–A♭–B♭	
	1–♭2–3–4–5–♭6–♭7	
Scale Harmonization:	C7	C–E–G–B♭
	D♭ma7	D♭–F–A♭–C
	E°7	E–G–B♭–D♭
	Fmi(ma7)	F–A♭–C–E
	Gmi7(♭5)	G–B♭–D♭–F
	A♭ma7(♯5)	A♭–C–E–G
	B♭mi7	B♭–D♭–F–A♭

The Ahavoh Rabboh scale is a harmonic minor scale starting on the 5th degree. It's very common in Middle Eastern music, and you can hear it played in modal compositions featuring a stringed instrument called the *oud* (lute). In Western music this scale can be played in styles that use processed guitar sounds like rock and jazz.

Example 1

This example utilizes two-note-per-string string-skipping over a C7 groove.

Example 2

Here's another example over C7. Notice the minor-3rd leap at the end of beat 2, which provides the characteristic harmonic minor sound.

Example 3

This example is over an E°7 funk groove and combines legato technique with a bit of string-skipping. The lick ends with a tart minor-2nd double stop.

Track 13

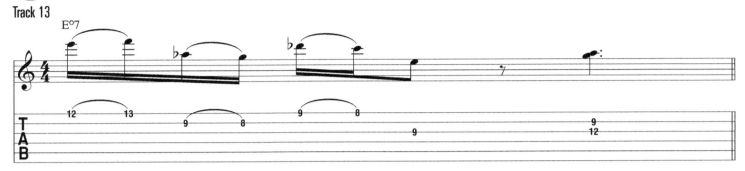

Example 4

Here, over the same E diminished funk groove, we're using an octave string-skipping lick and this time ending with a sus4 triad (F–B♭–C).

Track 14

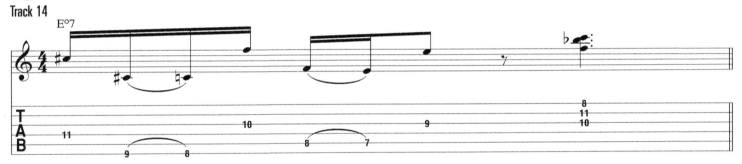

Example 5

Here's a series of double stops over E°7 using the Hebrew scale.

Track 15

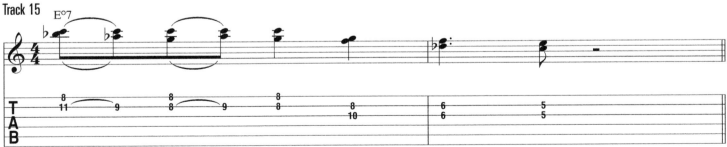

Hungarian Gypsy Minor Scale

The Scale:	A–B–C–D♯–E–F–G♯	
	1–2–♭3–♯4–5–♭6–7	
Scale Harmonization:	Ami(ma7)	A–C–E–G♯
	B7(♭5)	B–D♯–F–A
	Cma7(♯5)	C–E–G♯–B
	F7/D♯	D♯ (E♭)–F–A–C
	Ema7	E–G♯–B–D♯
	Fma7	F–A–C–E
	G♯mi6	G♯–B–D♯–F

The Hungarian gypsy minor scale can be seen as a harmonic minor scale with a ♯4 (or ♭5). Guitar players such as Jimmy and Stochello Rosenberg and Bireli Lagrene commonly use this scale in jazz gypsy music. Middle Eastern oud music also makes use of this scale. In their culture, the name of this scale is *nawa athar maqam* ("maqam" means mode in Middle Eastern music).

Example 1

This example demonstrates that the Hungarian gypsy minor scale works perfectly over an Ami7 Latin groove. Notice the melodic feel that the ♯4 (D♯) brings to the line.

Track 16

Example 2

This example uses the A Hungarian gypsy minor scale over an Ami7 funk groove.

Track 17

Example 3

Here's an ascending lick that's repeated in three octaves. It works very well over an Ami7 fusion groove.

Example 4

This example over an E–F progression has a Russian flavor. It uses string-skipping technique throughout.

Example 5

Here's another example of Russian guitar style with fast picking using A Hungarian minor.

Hindu Scale

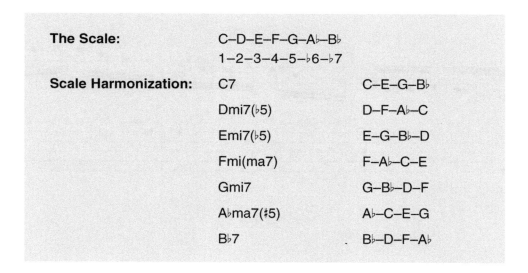

The Scale:	C–D–E–F–G–A♭–B♭	
	1–2–3–4–5–♭6–♭7	
Scale Harmonization:	C7	C–E–G–B♭
	Dmi7(♭5)	D–F–A♭–C
	Emi7(♭5)	E–G–B♭–D
	Fmi(ma7)	F–A♭–C–E
	Gmi7	G–B♭–D–F
	A♭ma7(♯5)	A♭–C–E–G
	B♭7	B♭–D–F–A♭

The Hindu scale is an F melodic minor scale starting on the 5th degree. It's also sometimes called Mixolydian ♭13.

Example 1

This is played over a C7–B♭7 progression. Anytime you have a C7, you can play the C Hindu scale. Notice that it contains both the 5th (G) and the ♯5th (G♯ or A♭). Because of this, the scale slightly resembles the whole-tone sound.

Track 21

Example 2

Here's what the scale sounds like sequenced in descending 3rds over the same progression.

Track 22

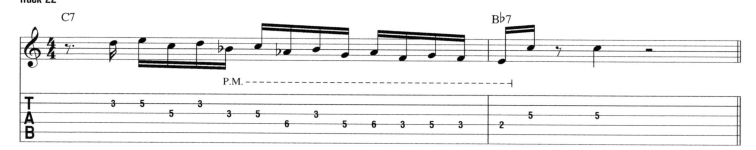

Example 3

Track 23

This example is over a Gmi7 funk-rock groove. Notice the nice tension produced by the A♭ at the end.

Example 4

Track 24

Here's how C Hindu sounds over Emi7(♭5).

Example 5

Track 25

Here's an Fmi6 arpeggio that combines sweeping technique with some slides over the Emi7(♭5) chord. Note that the C Hindu scale contains the notes of Fmi6, which are F, A♭, C, and D.

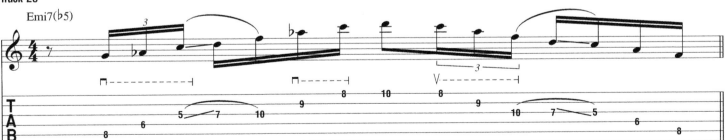

Neapolitan Major Scale

The Scale:	C–D♭–E♭–F–G–A–B	
	1–♭2–♭3–4–5–6–7	
Scale Harmonization:	Cmi(ma7)	C–E♭–G–B
	D♭ma7(♯5)	D♭–F–A–C
	E♭+7	E♭–G–B–D♭
	F7	F–A–C–E♭
	G7(♭5)	G–B–D♭–F
	Ami7(♭5)	A–C–E♭–G
	D♭+7/B	B (C♭)–D♭–F–A

The Neapolitan major scale can be seen as a melodic minor scale with a ♭2. You can also view this scale as a whole tone (D♭ whole tone in this case) with an added major 7th (C).

Example 1

This is played over Ami7(♭5). The Neapolitan major scale can create a melodic and intricate sound at the same time.

Track 26

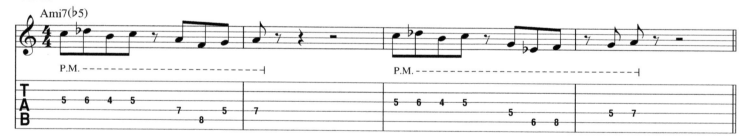

Example 2

This is also played over Ami7(♭5). Here we're using sixteenth notes at the fifth position with three notes per string.

Track 27

Example 3

 Here's another example of C Neapolitan major, but this time over F7.

Track 28   F7

Example 4

 You can start on any degree of the scale to create a melodic line. Here's another example over F7.

Track 29

Example 5

 Here's another melodic idea over F7 using the Neapolitan major scale.

Track 30   F7

Neapolitan Minor Scale

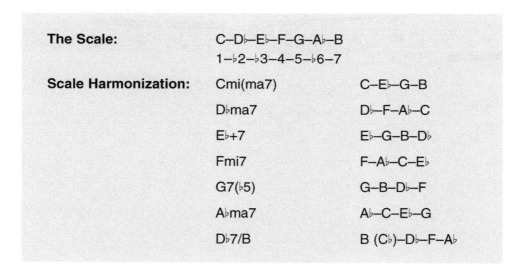

The Scale:	C–Db–Eb–F–G–Ab–B	
	1–b2–b3–4–5–b6–7	
Scale Harmonization:	Cmi(ma7)	C–Eb–G–B
	Dbma7	Db–F–Ab–C
	Eb+7	Eb–G–B–Db
	Fmi7	F–Ab–C–Eb
	G7(b5)	G–B–Db–F
	Abma7	Ab–C–Eb–G
	Db7/B	B (Cb)–Db–F–Ab

This scale can be seen as C Phrygian with a ♮7th (B), C harmonic minor with a b2nd, or Ab major with a #2nd (B).

Example 1

Track 31

This example is a straight-up Neapolitan minor line over an Fmi7 funk groove.

Example 2

Track 32

Here's another ascending Neapolitan minor idea over Fmi7.

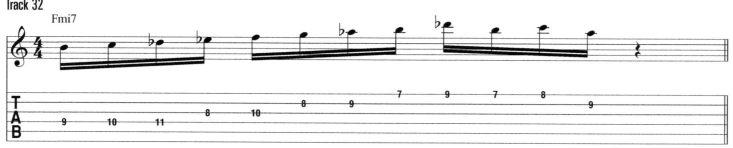

Example 3

Here's a descending idea over a faster Fmi7 funk groove.

Track 33

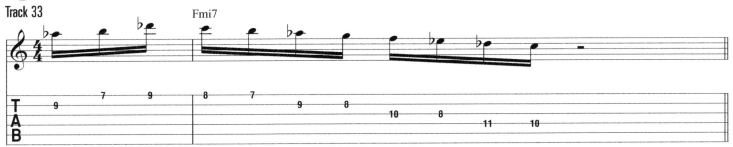

Example 4

This example uses octaves played with the pick and middle finger of the right hand.

Track 34

Example 5

Here's another idea with a Cajun funk groove over D♭ major and A♭ major.

Track 35

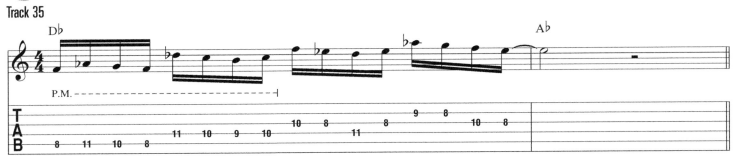

East Indian Scale (Raga Todi)

The Scale:	C–D♭–E♭–F♯–G–A♭–B	
	1–♭2–♭3–♯4–5–♭6–7	
Scale Harmonization:	Cmi(ma7)	C–E♭–G–B
	A♭7/D♭	D♭–F♯–A♭–C
	E♭+7	E♭–G–B–D♭
	A♭mi7	A♭–B (C♭)–E♭–F♯ (G♭)
	Gma7(♭5)	G–B–D♭–F♯
	A♭ma7	A♭–C–E♭–G
	B6/9(no3rd)	B–D♭–F♯–A♭

The C East Indian (Raga Todi) scale is an A♭ minor pentatonic scale with the additional C and G.

Example 1

Track 36

This example is over Cmi(ma7) with an Indian feel.

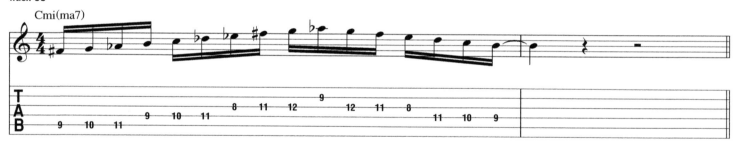

Example 2

Track 37

Here's an East Indian descending idea over Cmi(ma7).

Example 3

Track 38

Here's a chromatic idea using slides.

Cmi(ma7)

Example 4

Track 39

This is an extremely syncopated ascending line over an E♭+7 chord.

E♭+7

Example 5

Track 40

Here's another ascending line over E♭+7. Notice the ascending 4ths from string 5 to string 4.

E♭+7

Romanian Scale

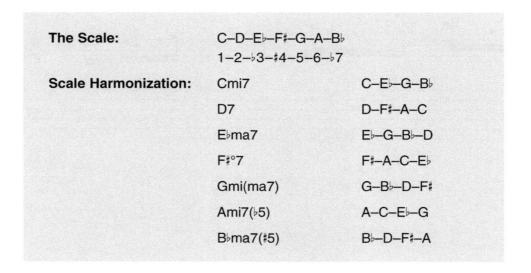

The Scale:	C–D–E♭–F♯–G–A–B♭	
	1–2–♭3–♯4–5–6–♭7	
Scale Harmonization:	Cmi7	C–E♭–G–B♭
	D7	D–F♯–A–C
	E♭ma7	E♭–G–B♭–D
	F♯°7	F♯–A–C–E♭
	Gmi(ma7)	G–B♭–D–F♯
	Ami7(♭5)	A–C–E♭–G
	B♭ma7(♯5)	B♭–D–F♯–A

The C Romanian scale is a G harmonic minor scale starting on the 4th degree.

Example 1

Here's a descending two-note-per-string pattern of the Romanian scale over Gmi(ma7).

Track 41

Example 2

Here's another melody using the Romanian scale over Gmi(ma7).

Track 42

Example 3

Track 43

This lick uses a mordent device (one fragment of a trill) over Ami7(♭5)–D7.

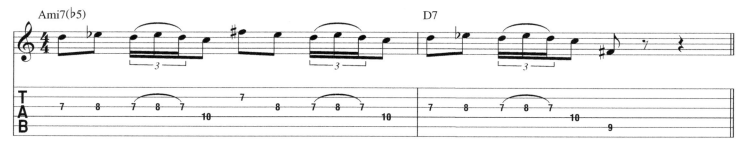

Example 4

Track 44

Here's a nice ascending lick using only the index and middle finger of the left hand over Ami7(♭5)–D7.

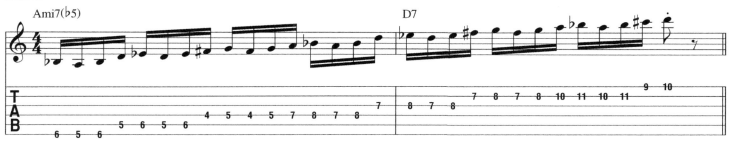

Example 5

Track 45

This is another lick using the index and middle finger. We're descending this time.

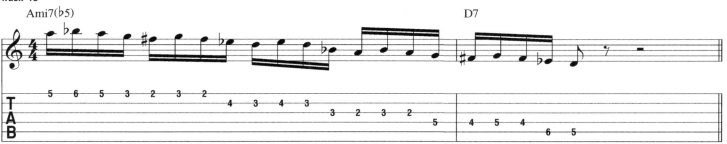

Double Harmonic Minor Scale

The Scale:	C–D♭–E–F–G–A♭–B	
	1–♭2–3–4–5–♭6–7	
Scale Harmonization:	Cma7	C–E–G–B
	D♭ma7	D♭–F–A♭–C
	Emi6	E–G–B–D♭
	Fmi(ma7)	F–A♭–C–E
	G7(♭5)	G–B–D♭–F
	A♭ma7(♯5)	A♭–C–E–G
	D♭7/B	B (C♭)–D♭–F–A♭

The C double harmonic minor scale is similar to F harmonic minor with a ♯4 (B).

Example 1

 Here's an example of the double harmonic minor scale over a D♭–C salsa groove.

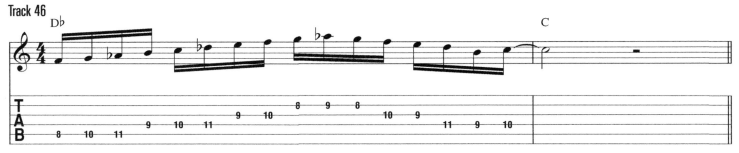

Example 2

This line repeats a six-note motive over the same groove.

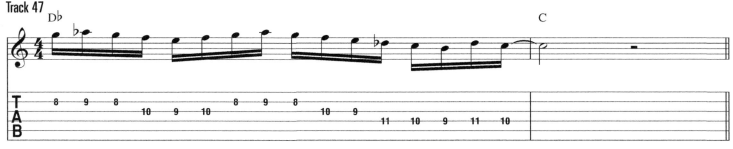

Example 3

Here we have a line that exploits the chromatic notes of the scale for a Santana-like sound.

Track 48

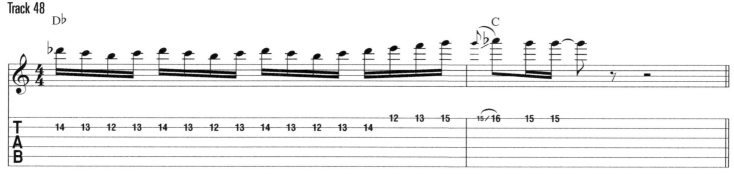

Example 4

Here's an idea using three and four notes per string over D♭–C.

Track 49

Example 5

This last example highlights the major 7th (C) over the D♭ chord.

Track 50

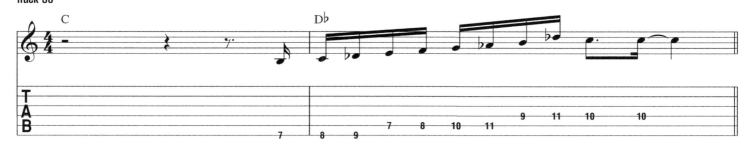

Persian Scale

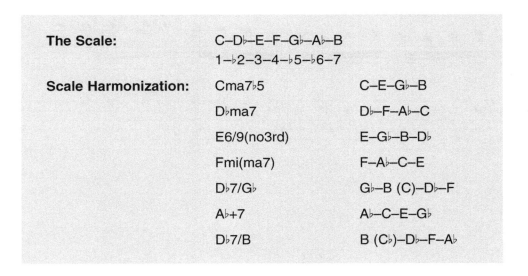

The Scale:	C–D♭–E–F–G♭–A♭–B	
	1–♭2–3–4–♭5–♭6–7	
Scale Harmonization:	Cma7♭5	C–E–G♭–B
	D♭ma7	D♭–F–A♭–C
	E6/9(no3rd)	E–G♭–B–D♭
	Fmi(ma7)	F–A♭–C–E
	D♭7/G♭	G♭–B (C)–D♭–F
	A♭+7	A♭–C–E–G♭
	D♭7/B	B (C♭)–D♭–F–A♭

The Persian scale is similar to the double harmonic minor scale, but it has a ♭5th (G♭).

Example 1

Here's a fast sixteenth-note example over Fmi(ma7) using the Persian scale.

Track 51

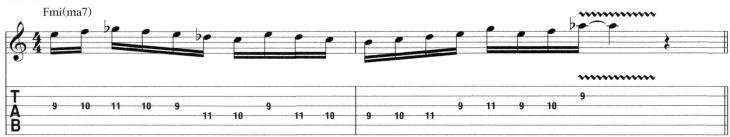

Example 2

In this example, we're repeating a twelve-note lick in a sixteenth-note rhythm.

Track 52

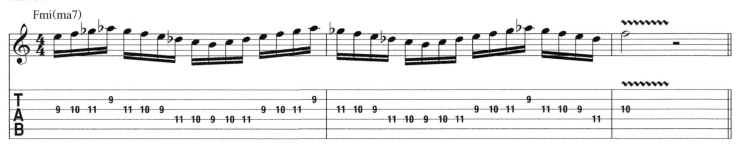

Example 3

Here's a nice string-skipping example. Notice the similar note groupings on the third and fourth strings.

Example 4

This line repeats a thirteen-note lick in a sixteenth-note rhythm using the Persian scale. Notice the unpredictable rhythmic effect created.

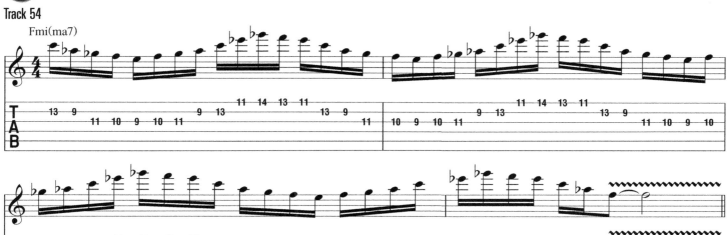

Example 5

Here's an eighth-note pedal tone idea using the Persian scale.

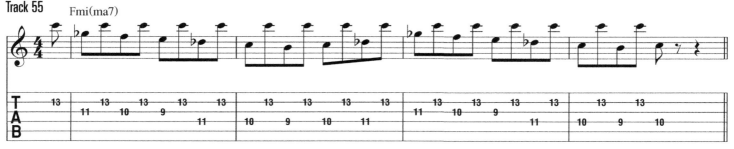

Double Augmented Scale

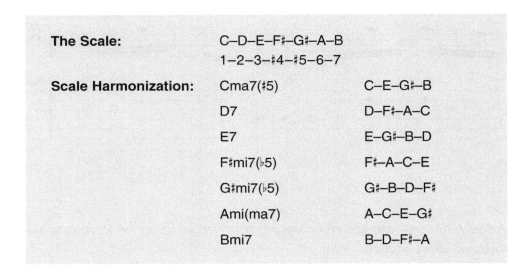

The Scale:	C–D–E–F♯–G♯–A–B	
	1–2–3–♯4–♯5–6–7	
Scale Harmonization:	Cma7(♯5)	C–E–G♯–B
	D7	D–F♯–A–C
	E7	E–G♯–B–D
	F♯mi7(♭5)	F♯–A–C–E
	G♯mi7(♭5)	G♯–B–D–F♯
	Ami(ma7)	A–C–E–G♯
	Bmi7	B–D–F♯–A

The C double augmented scale, also known as Lydian ♯5, is an A melodic minor scale starting on the 3rd degree.

Example 1

This is played over an E7–D7 shuffle groove. You can use C double augmented or A melodic minor. This string-skipping line is introduced by a bluesy open-string lick to set it up.

Track 56

Example 2

Here's another string-skipping idea over E7–D7. Notice how the triplet rhythm lends unpredictability to the rhythm.

Track 57

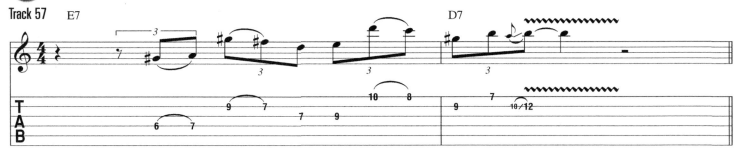

Example 3

Track 58

This example involves diatonic 4th intervals using sweeping technique in quintuplets!

Example 4

Track 59

This example is C double augmented over Bmi7 and uses string skipping.

Example 5

Track 60

Here's another lick over Bmi7 utilizing a three-octave pattern with four and two notes per string.

Eight-Tone Spanish Scale

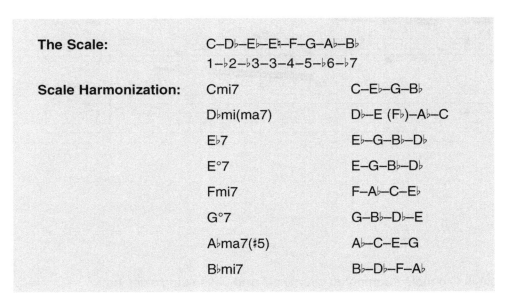

The Scale:	C–Db–Eb–E♮–F–G–Ab–Bb	
	1–b2–b3–3–4–5–b6–b7	
Scale Harmonization:	Cmi7	C–Eb–G–Bb
	Dbmi(ma7)	Db–E (Fb)–Ab–C
	Eb7	Eb–G–Bb–Db
	E°7	E–G–Bb–Db
	Fmi7	F–Ab–C–Eb
	G°7	G–Bb–Db–E
	Abma7(#5)	Ab–C–E–G
	Bbmi7	Bb–Db–F–Ab

The C eight-tone Spanish scale is an F harmonic minor scale with the addition of the b7th (Eb).

Example 1

Track 61

Here's an example using the C eight-tone Spanish scale with octaves over Dbmi(ma7).

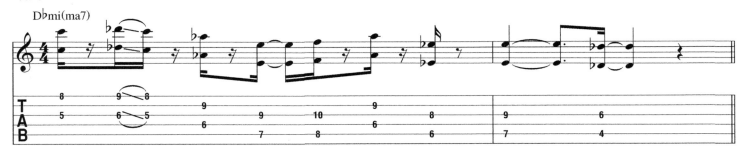

Example 2

Track 62

This example uses Dbmi, Cmi, and Fmi triads over Dbmi(ma7).

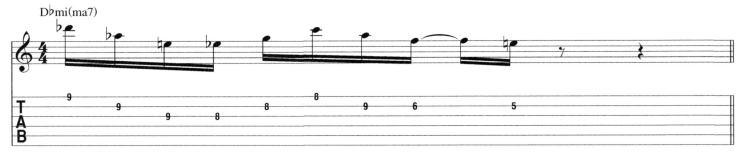

Example 3

Here's a syncopated lick that ends with an interesting repeated-note motive.

Track 63

Example 4

Here's another melodic idea using the C eight-tone Spanish scale.

Track 64

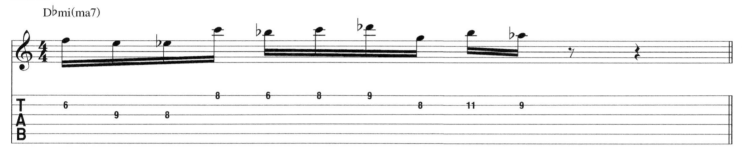

Example 5

This idea plays with the half-step intervals present in the scale.

Track 65

Byzantine Scale

The Scale:	C–D♭–E–F–G–A♭–B	
	1–♭2–3–4–5–♭6–7	
Scale Harmonization:	Cma7	C–E–G–B
	D♭ma7	D♭–F–A♭–C
	Emi6	E–G–B–D♭
	Fmi(ma7)	F–A♭–C–E
	G7♭5	G–B–D♭–F
	A♭ma7(♯5)	A♭–C–E–G
	D♭7/B	B (C♭)–D♭–F–A♭

The C Byzantine scale is similar to an F harmonic minor scale starting on the note C with the additional note B.

Example 1

Here's a fast lick played with four and three notes per string over a Cma7–D♭ma7 progression.

Example 2

This lick uses octaves and slides in a triplet rhythm over the same progression.

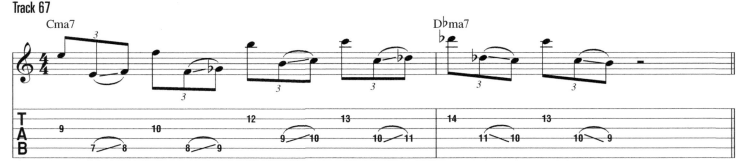

Example 3

Track 68

Here's a fast sixteenth-note ascending lick consisting of mostly half steps from the Byzantine scale.

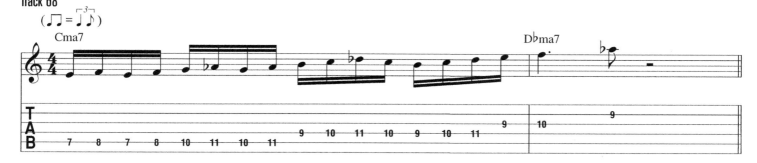

Example 4

Track 69

Here's a fast descending lick using four and three notes per string.

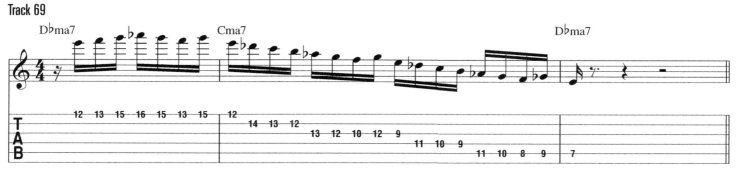

Example 5

Track 70

This line features descending triplets from the Byzantine scale, played in an ascending manner.

Overtone Scale

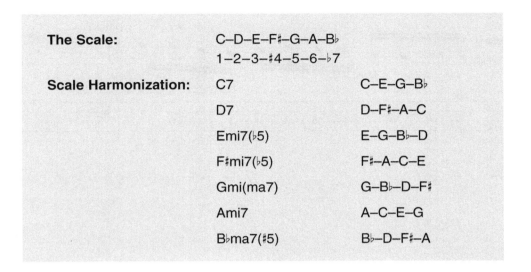

The Scale:	C–D–E–F♯–G–A–B♭	
	1–2–3–♯4–5–6–♭7	
Scale Harmonization:	C7	C–E–G–B♭
	D7	D–F♯–A–C
	Emi7(♭5)	E–G–B♭–D
	F♯mi7(♭5)	F♯–A–C–E
	Gmi(ma7)	G–B♭–D–F♯
	Ami7	A–C–E–G
	B♭ma7(♯5)	B♭–D–F♯–A

The C overtone scale is a G melodic minor scale starting on the 4th degree. It's also called the Bartok mode or Lydian ♭7 (by jazz musicians).

Example 1

 Here's an angular example of the C overtone scale over D7–C7.

Example 2

 This example is a bi-tonal lick using D augmented and C major triads over D7–C7.

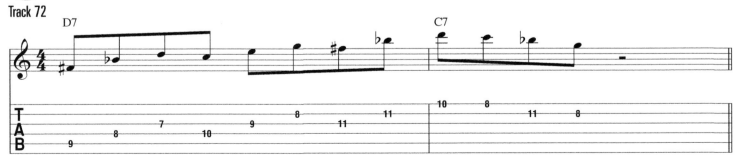

Example 3

 This lick expands on the previous concept, alternating D+ and C triads throughout.

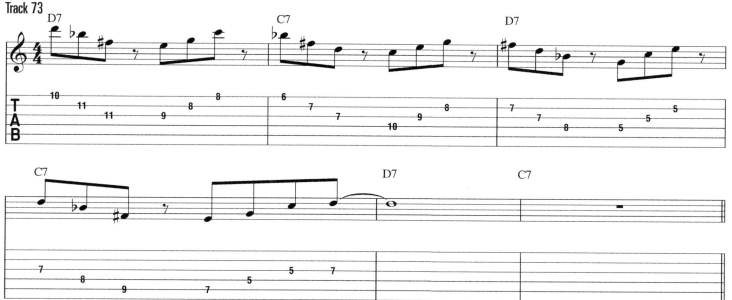

Example 4

 Here's a quicker version of the alternating triad concept in a triplet rhythm.

Example 5

 Here's another lick using three-note groupings, this time with the sweeping technique over Emi7(♭5).

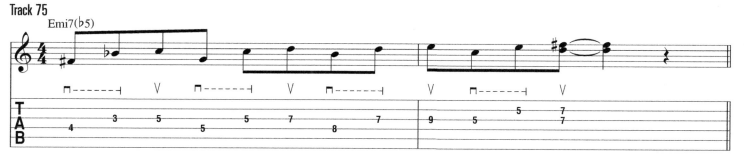

Harmonic Major Scale

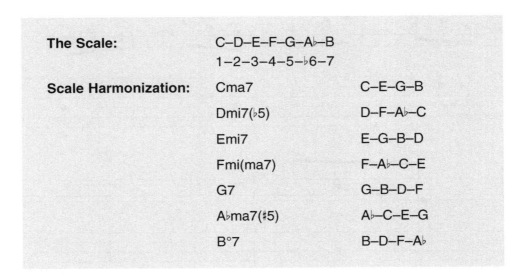

The Scale:	C–D–E–F–G–A♭–B	
	1–2–3–4–5–♭6–7	
Scale Harmonization:	Cma7	C–E–G–B
	Dmi7(♭5)	D–F–A♭–C
	Emi7	E–G–B–D
	Fmi(ma7)	F–A♭–C–E
	G7	G–B–D–F
	A♭ma7(♯5)	A♭–C–E–G
	B°7	B–D–F–A♭

The harmonic major scale is a harmonic minor scale with a major 3rd. Alternatively, you can think of it as a major scale with a ♭6th (A♭).

Example 1

Here's a syncopated example using the harmonic major scale over Cma7.

Track 76

Example 2

This example runs straight up through the scale in sixteenth notes over Cma7 before descending, so you get a good idea of its sound.

Track 77

Example 3

Track 78

Here's another ascending scalar idea using C harmonic major over Cma7–Dmi7(♭5)–G7.

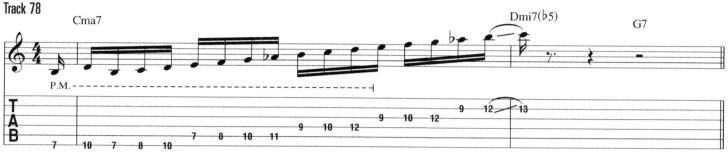

Example 4

This line runs up and down through the major scale and ends with a nice syncopated melody that highlights the ♭6th–5th scale degree movement of harmonic major in the Dmi7(♭5)–G7 progression.

Track 79

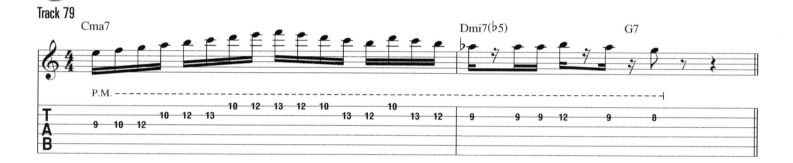

Example 5

Here's a sextuplet line that descends in groups of five, with harmonic major in the higher octave and major in the lower octave.

Track 80

MUSICIANS INSTITUTE ™

Musicians Institute Press is the official series of instructional publications from Southern California's renowned music school, Musicians Institute. These books, book/audio packages, and videos have been created by MI instructors who are among the world's best and most experienced professional musicians.

KEYBOARD

00695708	Blues Hanon by Peter Deneff	$17.99
00695556	Dictionary of Keyboard Grooves by Gail Johnson – Book/CD	$16.95
00202430	Easy Jazz Hanon by Peter Deneff – Book/Audio	$12.99
00695336	Funk Keyboards – The Complete Method by Gail Johnson – Book/Audio	$16.99
00695936	Hip-Hop Keyboard by Henry Soleh Brewer – Book/CD	$17.95
00695791	Jazz Chord Hanon by Peter Deneff	$17.99
00695554	Jazz Hanon by Peter Deneff	$16.99
00695773	Jazz Piano by Christian Klikovits – Book/CD	$19.99
00695209	Keyboard Voicings by Kevin King	$12.95
00266448	Modal Hanon by Peter Deneff	$14.99
00145419	Pop Keyboard Concepts by Christian Klikovits – Book/Audio	$19.99
00695509	Pop Rock Keyboards by Henry Sol-Eh Brewer & David Garfield – Book/CD	$19.95
00695784	Rock Hanon by Peter Deneff	$19.99
00695226	Salsa Hanon by Peter Deneff	$17.99
00695939	Samba Hanon by Peter Deneff	$16.99
00695882	Stride Hanon by Peter Deneff	$17.99

VOICE

00695883	Advanced Vocal Technique by Dena Murray and Tita Hutchison – Book/Audio	$19.99
00695262	Harmony Vocals by Mike Campbell & Tracee Lewis – Book/Audio	$19.99
00695626	The Musician's Guide to Recording Vocals by Dallan Beck – Book/CD	$15.99
00695629	Rock Vocals by Coreen Sheehan – Book/CD	$17.99
00695195	Sightsinging by Mike Campbell	$19.99
00695427	Vocal Technique by Dena Murray – Book/Audio	$24.99

GUITAR

00695922	Acoustic Artistry by Evan Hirschelman – Book/Audio	$19.99
00695298	Advanced Scale Concepts and Licks for Guitar by Jean Marc Belkadi – Book/CD	$17.99
00217709	All-in-One Guitar Soloing Course by Daniel Gilbert & Beth Marlis	$29.99
00695132	Blues Guitar Soloing by Keith Wyatt – Book/Online Media	$24.99
00695680	Blues/Rock Soloing for Guitar by Robert Calva – Book/Audio	$19.99
00695131	Blues Rhythm Guitar by Keith Wyatt – Book/Audio	$19.99
00696002	Modern Techniques for the Electric Guitarist by Dean Brown – DVD	$29.95
00695664	Chord Progressions for Guitar by Tom Kolb – Book/CD	$17.99
00695855	Chord Tone Soloing by Barrett Tagliarino – Book/Audio	$24.99
00695646	Chord-Melody Guitar by Bruce Buckingham – Book/CD	$19.99
00695171	Classical & Fingerstyle Guitar Techniques by David Oakes – Book/Audio	$17.99
00695806	Classical Themes for Electric Guitar by Jean Marc Belkadi – Book/CD	$15.99
00695661	Country Guitar by Al Bonhomme – Book/Audio	$19.99

00695227	The Diminished Scale for Guitar by Jean Marc Belkadi – Book/CD	$14.99
00695181	Essential Rhythm Guitar by Steve Trovato – Book/CD	$15.99
00695873	Ethnic Rhythms for Electric Guitar by Jean Marc Belkadi – Book/CD	$17.99
00695860	Exotic Scales & Licks for Electric Guitar by Jean Marc Belkadi – Book/CD	$16.95
00695419	Funk Guitar by Ross Bolton – Book/Audio	$15.99
00695134	Guitar Basics by Bruce Buckingham – Book/Audio	$17.99
00695712	Guitar Fretboard Workbook by Barrett Tagliarino	$19.99
00695321	Guitar Hanon by Peter Deneff	$14.99
00695482	The Guitar Lick•tionary by Dave Hill – Book/CD	$19.99
00695190	Guitar Soloing by Daniel Gilbert and Beth Marlis – Book/Audio	$22.99
00695169	Harmonics by Jamie Findlay – Book/CD	$13.99
00695406	Introduction to Jazz Guitar Soloing by Joe Elliott – Book/Audio	$19.95
00695291	Jazz Guitar Chord System by Scott Henderson	$12.99
00217711	Jazz Guitar Improvisation by Sid Jacobs – Book/Online Media	$19.99
00217690	Jazz, Rock & Funk Guitar by Dean Brown – Book/Online Media	$19.99
00695361	Jazz-Rock Triad Improvising for Guitar by Jean Marc Belkadi – Book/CD	$15.99
00695379	Latin Guitar by Bruce Buckingham – Book/Audio	$17.99
00696656	Liquid Legato by Allen Hinds – Book/CD	$14.99
00695143	A Modern Approach to Jazz, Rock & Fusion Guitar by Jean Marc Belkadi – Book/CD	$15.99
00695711	Modern Jazz Concepts for Guitar by Sid Jacobs – Book/CD	$16.95
00695682	Modern Rock Rhythm Guitar by Danny Gill – Book/CD	$16.95
00695555	Modes for Guitar by Tom Kolb – Book/Audio	$18.99
00695192	Music Reading for Guitar by David Oakes	$19.99
00695697	Outside Guitar Licks by Jean Marc Belkadi – Book/CD	$16.99
00695962	Power Plucking by Dale Turner – Book/CD	$19.95
00695748	Progressive Tapping Licks by Jean Marc Belkadi – Book/CD	$16.99
00114559	Rhythm Guitar by Bruce Buckingham & Eric Paschal – Book/Audio	$24.99
00695188	Rhythm Guitar by Bruce Buckingham & Eric Paschal – Book	$19.99
00695909	Rhythm Guitar featuring Bruce Buckingham – DVD	$19.95
00110263	Rhythmic Lead Guitar by Barrett Tagliarino – Book/Audio	$19.99
00695144	Rock Lead Basics by Nick Nolan and Danny Gill – Book/Audio	$18.99
00695278	Rock Lead Performance by Nick Nolan and Danny Gill – Book/Audio	$17.99
00695146	Rock Lead Techniques by Nick Nolan and Danny Gill – Book/Audio	$16.99
00695977	Shred Guitar by Greg Harrison – Book/Audio	$19.99
00139556	Solo Slap Guitar by Jude Gold – Book/Video	$19.99
00695645	Slap & Pop Technique for Guitar by Jean Marc Belkadi – Book/CD	$16.99
00695913	Technique Exercises for Guitar by Jean Marc Belkadi – Book/CD	$15.99
00695340	Texas Blues Guitar by Robert Calva – Book/Audio	$17.99
00695863	Ultimate Guitar Technique by Bill LaFleur – Book/Audio	$22.99

BASS

00695133	Arpeggios for Bass by David Keif	$14.95
00695168	The Art of Walking Bass by Bob Magnusson – Book/Audio	$19.99
00696026	Bass Blueprints by Dominik Hauser – Book/CD	$18.99
00695201	Bass Fretboard Basics by Paul Farnen	$17.99
00695207	Bass Playing Techniques by Alexis Sklarevski	$17.99
00696191	Beginning Jazz Bass by Dominick Hauser – Book/Audio	$19.99
00695934	Chords for Bass by Dominik Hauser – Book/Audio	$17.99
00695771	Groove Mastery by Oneida James – Book/CD	$17.95
00695265	Grooves for Electric Bass by David Keif – Book/CD	$16.99
00696413	Jazz Bass Improvisation by Putter Smith – Book/CD	$16.99
00695543	Latin Bass by George Lopez & David Keif – Book/CD	$16.99
00695203	Music Reading for Bass by Wendi Hrehhovcsik	$14.99
00696371	Progressive Rock Bass by Christopher Maloney – Book/CD	$19.99
00696411	Soloing for Bass Master Class by Dominik Hauser – Book/CD	$19.99

DRUMS

00695328	Afro-Cuban Coordination for Drumset by Maria Martinez – Book/Audio	$16.99
00695623	Blues Drumming by Ed Roscetti – Book/CD	$17.99
00695284	Brazilian Coordination for Drumset by Maria Martinez – Book/CD	$15.99
00695129	Chart Reading Workbook for Drummers by Bobby Gabriele – Book/CD	$16.99
00695349	Drummer's Guide to Odd Meters by Ed Roscetti – Book/CD	$15.99
00217738	Essential Double Bass Drumming Techniques by Jeff Bowders – Book/Online Media	$24.99
00695986	Essential Drumset Fills by Jeff Bowders – Book/Audio	$19.99
00696622	Essential Rock Drumming Concepts by Jeff Bowders – Book/CD	$24.99
00695679	Funk & Hip-Hop Drumming by Ed Roscetti – Book/CD	$17.99
00129581	Jazz Drumming by Donny Gruendler – Book/Audio	$19.99
00695287	Latin Soloing for Drumset by Phil Maturano – Book/Audio	$16.99
00126961	Ray Luzier's Double Bass Drum Techniques – Book/Video	$29.99
00695876	Ray Luzier – DVD	$29.95
00695838	Rock Drumming Workbook by Ed Roscetti – Book/CD	$19.95
00695127	Working the Inner Clock for Drumset by Phil Maturano – Book/CD	$19.99

ALL INSTRUMENTS/OTHER

00695135	An Approach to Jazz Improvisation by Dave Pozzi – Book/CD	$17.95
00128943	DJ Techniques – Vinyl and Digital by Charlie Sputnik	$19.99
00695198	Ear Training by Keith Wyatt, Carl Schroeder and Joe Elliott – Book/Audio	$24.99
00695145	Encyclopedia of Reading Rhythms by Gary Hess	$24.99
00695161	Harmony and Theory by Keith Wyatt and Carl Schroeder	$19.99
00695130	Lead Sheet Bible by Robin Randall and Janice Peterson – Book/CD	$19.95

RECORDING

| 00113117 | Essential Guide to Songwriting, Producing & Recording by Darryl Swann | $16.99 |
| 00695626 | The Musician's Guide to Recording Vocals by Dallan Beck – Book/CD | $15.99 |

www.halleonard.com

Prices, contents and availability subject to change without notice.

GUITAR *signature licks*

Signature Licks book/audio packs provide a step-by-step breakdown of "right from the record" riffs, licks, and solos so you can jam along with your favorite bands. They contain performance notes and an overview of each artist's or group's style, with note-for-note transcriptions in notes and tab. The CDs or online audio tracks feature full-band demos at both normal and slow speeds.

AC/DC
14041352 .... $22.99

AEROSMITH 1973-1979
00695106 .... $22.95

AEROSMITH 1979-1998
00695219 .... $22.95

DUANE ALLMAN
00696042 .... $22.99

BEST OF CHET ATKINS
00695752 .... $24.99

AVENGED SEVENFOLD
00696473 .... $22.99

BEST OF THE BEATLES FOR ACOUSTIC GUITAR
00695453 .... $22.99

THE BEATLES BASS
00695283 .... $22.99

THE BEATLES FAVORITES
00695096 .... $24.95

THE BEATLES HITS
00695049 .... $24.95

JEFF BECK
00696427 .... $22.99

BEST OF GEORGE BENSON
00695418 .... $22.99

BEST OF BLACK SABBATH
00695249 .... $22.95

BLUES BREAKERS WITH JOHN MAYALL & ERIC CLAPTON
00696374 .... $22.99

BON JOVI
00696380 .... $22.99

ROY BUCHANAN
00696654 .... $22.99

KENNY BURRELL
00695830 .... $24.99

BEST OF CHARLIE CHRISTIAN
00695584 .... $22.95

BEST OF ERIC CLAPTON
00695038 .... $24.99

ERIC CLAPTON – FROM THE ALBUM UNPLUGGED
00695250 .... $24.95

BEST OF CREAM
00695251 .... $22.95

CREEDANCE CLEARWATER REVIVAL
00695924 .... $22.95

DEEP PURPLE – GREATEST HITS
00695625 .... $22.99

THE BEST OF DEF LEPPARD
00696516 .... $22.99

DREAM THEATER
00111943 .... $24.99

TOMMY EMMANUEL
00696409 .... $22.99

ESSENTIAL JAZZ GUITAR
00695875 .... $19.99

FAMOUS ROCK GUITAR SOLOS
00695590 .... $19.95

FLEETWOOD MAC
00696416 .... $22.99

BEST OF FOO FIGHTERS
00695481 .... $24.95

ROBBEN FORD
00695903 .... $22.95

BEST OF GRANT GREEN
00695747 .... $22.99

PETER GREEN
00145386 .... $22.99

THE GUITARS OF ELVIS – 2ND ED.
00174800 .... $22.99

BEST OF GUNS N' ROSES
00695183 .... $24.99

THE BEST OF BUDDY GUY
00695186 .... $22.99

JIM HALL
00695848 .... $24.99

JIMI HENDRIX
00696560 .... $24.99

JIMI HENDRIX – VOLUME 2
00695835 .... $24.99

JOHN LEE HOOKER
00695894 .... $19.99

BEST OF JAZZ GUITAR
00695586 .... $24.95

ERIC JOHNSON
00699317 .... $24.99

ROBERT JOHNSON
00695264 .... $22.95

BARNEY KESSEL
00696009 .... $24.99

THE ESSENTIAL ALBERT KING
00695713 .... $22.95

B.B. KING – BLUES LEGEND
00696039 .... $22.99

B.B. KING – THE DEFINITIVE COLLECTION
00695635 .... $22.95

B.B. KING – MASTER BLUESMAN
00699923 .... $24.99

MARK KNOPFLER
00695178 .... $24.99

LYNYRD SKYNYRD
00695872 .... $24.99

THE BEST OF YNGWIE MALMSTEEN
00695669 .... $22.95

BEST OF PAT MARTINO
00695632 .... $24.99

MEGADETH
00696421 .... $22.99

WES MONTGOMERY
00695387 .... $24.99

BEST OF NIRVANA
00695483 .... $24.95

VERY BEST OF OZZY OSBOURNE
00695431 .... $22.99

BRAD PAISLEY
00696379 .... $22.99

BEST OF JOE PASS
00695730 .... $22.99

JACO PASTORIUS
00695544 .... $24.95

TOM PETTY
00696021 .... $22.99

PINK FLOYD
00103659 .... $24.99

BEST OF QUEEN
00695097 .... $24.99

RADIOHEAD
00109304 .... $24.99

BEST OF RAGE AGAINST THE MACHINE
00695480 .... $24.95

RED HOT CHILI PEPPERS
00695173 .... $22.95

RED HOT CHILI PEPPERS – GREATEST HITS
00695828 .... $24.99

JERRY REED
00118236 .... $22.99

BEST OF DJANGO REINHARDT
00695660 .... $24.99

BEST OF ROCK 'N' ROLL GUITAR
00695559 .... $22.99

BEST OF ROCKABILLY GUITAR
00695785 .... $19.95

BEST OF CARLOS SANTANA
00174664 .... $22.99

BEST OF JOE SATRIANI
00695216 .... $22.95

SLASH
00696576 .... $22.99

SLAYER
00121281 .... $22.99

THE BEST OF SOUL GUITAR
00695703 .... $19.95

BEST OF SOUTHERN ROCK
00695560 .... $19.95

STEELY DAN
00696015 .... $22.99

MIKE STERN
00695800 .... $24.99

BEST OF SURF GUITAR
00695822 .... $19.99

STEVE VAI
00673247 .... $22.95

STEVE VAI – ALIEN LOVE SECRETS: THE NAKED VAMPS
00695223 .... $22.95

STEVE VAI – FIRE GARDEN: THE NAKED VAMPS
00695166 .... $22.95

STEVE VAI – THE ULTRA ZONE: NAKED VAMPS
00695684 .... $22.95

VAN HALEN
00110227 .... $24.99

STEVIE RAY VAUGHAN – 2ND ED.
00699316 .... $24.95

THE GUITAR STYLE OF STEVIE RAY VAUGHAN
00695155 .... $24.95

BEST OF THE VENTURES
00695772 .... $19.95

THE WHO – 2ND ED.
00695561 .... $22.95

JOHNNY WINTER
00695951 .... $22.99

YES
00113120 .... $22.99

NEIL YOUNG – GREATEST HITS
00695988 .... $22.99

BEST OF ZZ TOP
00695738 .... $24.95

HAL•LEONARD®

www.halleonard.com

COMPLETE DESCRIPTIONS AND SONGLISTS ONLINE!
Prices, contents and availability subject to change without notice.

HAL•LEONARD® GUITAR PLAY-ALONG

AUDIO ACCESS INCLUDED

This series will help you play your favorite songs quickly and easily. Just follow the tab and listen to the audio to the hear how the guitar should sound, and then play along using the separate backing tracks. Audio files also include software to slow down the tempo without changing pitch. The melody and lyrics are included in the book so that you can sing or simply follow along.

INCLUDES TAB

VOL. 1 – ROCK	00699570 / $16.99
VOL. 2 – ACOUSTIC	00699569 / $16.99
VOL. 3 – HARD ROCK	00699573 / $17.99
VOL. 4 – POP/ROCK	00699571 / $16.99
VOL. 6 – '90S ROCK	00699572 / $16.99
VOL. 7 – BLUES	00699575 / $17.99
VOL. 8 – ROCK	00699585 / $16.99
VOL. 9 – EASY ACOUSTIC SONGS	00151708 / $16.99
VOL. 10 – ACOUSTIC	00699586 / $16.95
VOL. 13 – FOLK ROCK	00699581 / $16.99
VOL. 14 – BLUES ROCK	00699582 / $16.99
VOL. 15 – R&B	00699583 / $16.99
VOL. 16 – JAZZ	00699584 / $15.95
VOL. 17 – COUNTRY	00699588 / $16.99
VOL. 18 – ACOUSTIC ROCK	00699577 / $15.95
VOL. 20 – ROCKABILLY	00699580 / $16.99
VOL. 21 – SANTANA	00174525 / $17.99
VOL. 22 – CHRISTMAS	00699600 / $15.99
VOL. 23 – SURF	00699635 / $15.99
VOL. 24 – ERIC CLAPTON	00699649 / $17.99
VOL. 25 – THE BEATLES	00198265 / $17.99
VOL. 26 – ELVIS PRESLEY	00699643 / $16.99
VOL. 27 – DAVID LEE ROTH	00699645 / $16.95
VOL. 28 – GREG KOCH	00699646 / $17.99
VOL. 29 – BOB SEGER	00699647 / $16.99
VOL. 30 – KISS	00699644 / $16.99
VOL. 32 – THE OFFSPRING	00699653 / $14.95
VOL. 33 – ACOUSTIC CLASSICS	00699656 / $17.99
VOL. 34 – CLASSIC ROCK	00699658 / $17.99
VOL. 35 – HAIR METAL	00699660 / $17.99
VOL. 36 – SOUTHERN ROCK	00699661 / $17.99
VOL. 37 – ACOUSTIC UNPLUGGED	00699662 / $22.99
VOL. 38 – BLUES	00699663 / $16.95
VOL. 39 – '80S METAL	00699664 / $16.99
VOL. 40 – INCUBUS	00699668 / $17.95
VOL. 41 – ERIC CLAPTON	00699669 / $17.99
VOL. 42 – COVER BAND HITS	00211597 / $16.99
VOL. 43 – LYNYRD SKYNYRD	00699681 / $17.99
VOL. 44 – JAZZ	00699689 / $16.99
VOL. 45 – TV THEMES	00699718 / $14.95
VOL. 46 – MAINSTREAM ROCK	00699722 / $16.95
VOL. 47 – HENDRIX SMASH HITS	00699723 / $19.99
VOL. 48 – AEROSMITH CLASSICS	00699724 / $17.99
VOL. 49 – STEVIE RAY VAUGHAN	00699725 / $17.99
VOL. 50 – VAN HALEN 1978-1984	00110269 / $17.99
VOL. 51 – ALTERNATIVE '90S	00699727 / $14.99
VOL. 52 – FUNK	00699728 / $15.99
VOL. 53 – DISCO	00699729 / $14.99
VOL. 54 – HEAVY METAL	00699730 / $16.99
VOL. 55 – POP METAL	00699731 / $14.95
VOL. 56 – FOO FIGHTERS	00699749 / $17.99
VOL. 59 – CHET ATKINS	00702347 / $16.99
VOL. 62 – CHRISTMAS CAROLS	00699798 / $12.95
VOL. 63 – CREEDENCE CLEARWATER REVIVAL	00699802 / $16.99
VOL. 64 – THE ULTIMATE OZZY OSBOURNE	00699803 / $17.99
VOL. 66 – THE ROLLING STONES	00699807 / $17.99
VOL. 67 – BLACK SABBATH	00699808 / $16.99
VOL. 68 – PINK FLOYD – DARK SIDE OF THE MOON	00699809 / $16.99
VOL. 70 – OZZY OSBOURNE	00699805 / $16.99
VOL. 73 – BLUESY ROCK	00699829 / $16.99
VOL. 74 – SIMPLE STRUMMING SONGS	00151706 / $19.99

VOL. 75 – TOM PETTY	00699882 / $16.99
VOL. 76 – COUNTRY HITS	00699884 / $16.99
VOL. 77 – BLUEGRASS	00699910 / $15.99
VOL. 78 – NIRVANA	00700132 / $16.99
VOL. 79 – NEIL YOUNG	00700133 / $24.99
VOL. 80 – ACOUSTIC ANTHOLOGY	00700175 / $19.95
VOL. 81 – ROCK ANTHOLOGY	00700176 / $22.99
VOL. 82 – EASY SONGS	00700177 / $16.99
VOL. 84 – STEELY DAN	00700200 / $17.99
VOL. 85 – THE POLICE	00700269 / $16.99
VOL. 86 – BOSTON	00700465 / $16.99
VOL. 87 – ACOUSTIC WOMEN	00700763 / $14.99
VOL. 89 – REGGAE	00700468 / $15.99
VOL. 90 – CLASSICAL POP	00700469 / $14.99
VOL. 91 – BLUES INSTRUMENTALS	00700505 / $15.99
VOL. 92 – EARLY ROCK INSTRUMENTALS	00700506 / $15.99
VOL. 93 – ROCK INSTRUMENTALS	00700507 / $16.99
VOL. 94 – SLOW BLUES	00700508 / $16.99
VOL. 95 – BLUES CLASSICS	00700509 / $15.99
VOL. 96 – BEST COUNTRY HITS	00211615 / $16.99
VOL. 97 – CHRISTMAS CLASSICS	00236542 / $14.99
VOL. 99 – ZZ TOP	00700762 / $16.99
VOL. 100 – B.B. KING	00700466 / $16.99
VOL. 101 – SONGS FOR BEGINNERS	00701917 / $14.99
VOL. 102 – CLASSIC PUNK	00700769 / $14.99
VOL. 103 – SWITCHFOOT	00700773 / $16.99
VOL. 104 – DUANE ALLMAN	00700846 / $16.99
VOL. 105 – LATIN	00700939 / $16.99
VOL. 106 – WEEZER	00700958 / $14.99
VOL. 107 – CREAM	00701069 / $16.99
VOL. 108 – THE WHO	00701053 / $16.99
VOL. 109 – STEVE MILLER	00701054 / $19.99
VOL. 110 – SLIDE GUITAR HITS	00701055 / $16.99
VOL. 111 – JOHN MELLENCAMP	00701056 / $14.99
VOL. 112 – QUEEN	00701052 / $16.99
VOL. 113 – JIM CROCE	00701058 / $17.99
VOL. 114 – BON JOVI	00701060 / $16.99
VOL. 115 – JOHNNY CASH	00701070 / $16.99
VOL. 116 – THE VENTURES	00701124 / $16.99
VOL. 117 – BRAD PAISLEY	00701224 / $16.99
VOL. 118 – ERIC JOHNSON	00701353 / $16.99
VOL. 119 – AC/DC CLASSICS	00701356 / $17.99
VOL. 120 – PROGRESSIVE ROCK	00701457 / $14.99
VOL. 121 – U2	00701508 / $16.99
VOL. 122 – CROSBY, STILLS & NASH	00701610 / $16.99
VOL. 123 – LENNON & MCCARTNEY ACOUSTIC	00701614 / $16.99
VOL. 125 – JEFF BECK	00701687 / $16.99
VOL. 126 – BOB MARLEY	00701701 / $16.99
VOL. 127 – 1970S ROCK	00701739 / $16.99
VOL. 128 – 1960S ROCK	00701740 / $14.99
VOL. 129 – MEGADETH	00701741 / $17.99
VOL. 130 – IRON MAIDEN	00701742 / $17.99
VOL. 131 – 1990S ROCK	00701743 / $14.99
VOL. 132 – COUNTRY ROCK	00701757 / $15.99
VOL. 133 – TAYLOR SWIFT	00701894 / $16.99
VOL. 134 – AVENGED SEVENFOLD	00701906 / $16.99
VOL. 135 – MINOR BLUES	00151350 / $17.99
VOL. 136 – GUITAR THEMES	00701922 / $14.99
VOL. 137 – IRISH TUNES	00701966 / $15.99
VOL. 138 – BLUEGRASS CLASSICS	00701967 / $16.99
VOL. 139 – GARY MOORE	00702370 / $16.99
VOL. 140 – MORE STEVIE RAY VAUGHAN	00702396 / $17.99
VOL. 141 – ACOUSTIC HITS	00702401 / $16.99

VOL. 142 – GEORGE HARRISON	00237697 / $17.99
VOL. 143 – SLASH	00702425 / $19.99
VOL. 144 – DJANGO REINHARDT	00702531 / $16.99
VOL. 145 – DEF LEPPARD	00702532 / $17.99
VOL. 146 – ROBERT JOHNSON	00702533 / $16.99
VOL. 147 – SIMON & GARFUNKEL	14041591 / $16.99
VOL. 148 – BOB DYLAN	14041592 / $16.99
VOL. 149 – AC/DC HITS	14041593 / $17.99
VOL. 150 – ZAKK WYLDE	02501717 / $16.99
VOL. 151 – J.S. BACH	02501730 / $16.99
VOL. 152 – JOE BONAMASSA	02501751 / $19.99
VOL. 153 – RED HOT CHILI PEPPERS	00702990 / $19.99
VOL. 155 – ERIC CLAPTON – FROM THE ALBUM UNPLUGGED	00703085 / $16.99
VOL. 156 – SLAYER	00703770 / $17.99
VOL. 157 – FLEETWOOD MAC	00101382 / $16.99
VOL. 159 – WES MONTGOMERY	00102593 / $19.99
VOL. 160 – T-BONE WALKER	00102641 / $17.99
VOL. 161 – THE EAGLES – ACOUSTIC	00102659 / $17.99
VOL. 162 – THE EAGLES HITS	00102667 / $17.99
VOL. 163 – PANTERA	00103036 / $17.99
VOL. 164 – VAN HALEN 1986-1995	00110270 / $17.99
VOL. 165 – GREEN DAY	00210343 / $17.99
VOL. 166 – MODERN BLUES	00700764 / $16.99
VOL. 167 – DREAM THEATER	00111938 / $24.99
VOL. 168 – KISS	00113421 / $17.99
VOL. 169 – TAYLOR SWIFT	00115982 / $16.99
VOL. 170 – THREE DAYS GRACE	00117337 / $16.99
VOL. 171 – JAMES BROWN	00117420 / $16.99
VOL. 172 – THE DOOBIE BROTHERS	00119670 / $16.99
VOL. 173 – TRANS-SIBERIAN ORCHESTRA	00119907 / $19.99
VOL. 174 – SCORPIONS	00122119 / $16.99
VOL. 175 – MICHAEL SCHENKER	00122127 / $16.99
VOL. 176 – BLUES BREAKERS WITH JOHN MAYALL & ERIC CLAPTON	00122132 / $19.99
VOL. 177 – ALBERT KING	00123271 / $16.99
VOL. 178 – JASON MRAZ	00124165 / $17.99
VOL. 179 – RAMONES	00127073 / $16.99
VOL. 180 – BRUNO MARS	00129706 / $16.99
VOL. 181 – JACK JOHNSON	00129854 / $16.99
VOL. 182 – SOUNDGARDEN	00138161 / $17.99
VOL. 183 – BUDDY GUY	00138240 / $17.99
VOL. 184 – KENNY WAYNE SHEPHERD	00138258 / $17.99
VOL. 185 – JOE SATRIANI	00139457 / $17.99
VOL. 186 – GRATEFUL DEAD	00139459 / $17.99
VOL. 187 – JOHN DENVER	00140839 / $17.99
VOL. 188 – MÖTLEY CRUE	00141145 / $17.99
VOL. 189 – JOHN MAYER	00144350 / $17.99
VOL. 190 – DEEP PURPLE	00146152 / $17.99
VOL. 191 – PINK FLOYD CLASSICS	00146164 / $17.99
VOL. 192 – JUDAS PRIEST	00151352 / $17.99
VOL. 193 – STEVE VAI	00156028 / $19.99
VOL. 195 – METALLICA: 1983-1988	00234291 / $19.99
VOL. 196 – METALLICA: 1991-2016	00234292 / $19.99

Prices, contents, and availability subject to change without notice.

Complete song lists available online.

HAL•LEONARD®
www.halleonard.com

0319
173

Get Better at Guitar

...with these Great Guitar Instruction Books from Hal Leonard!

101 GUITAR TIPS
INCLUDES TAB

STUFF ALL THE PROS KNOW AND USE

by Adam St. James

This book contains invaluable guidance on everything from scales and music theory to truss rod adjustments, proper recording studio set-ups, and much more. The book also features snippets of advice from some of the most celebrated guitarists and producers in the music business, including B.B. King, Steve Vai, Joe Satriani, Warren Haynes, Laurence Juber, Pete Anderson, Tom Dowd and others, culled from the author's hundreds of interviews.

00695737 Book/Online Audio $16.99

AMAZING PHRASING
INCLUDES TAB

50 WAYS TO IMPROVE YOUR IMPROVISATIONAL SKILLS

by Tom Kolb

This book/audio pack explores all the main components necessary for crafting well-balanced rhythmic and melodic phrases. It also explains how these phrases are put together to form cohesive solos. Many styles are covered – rock, blues, jazz, fusion, country, Latin, funk and more – and all of the concepts are backed up with musical examples. The companion audio contains 89 demos for listening, and most tracks feature full-band backing.

00695583 Book/Online Audio $19.99

BLUES YOU CAN USE – 2ND EDITION

by John Ganapes

This comprehensive source for learning blues guitar is designed to develop both your lead and rhythm playing. Includes: 21 complete solos • blues chords, progressions and riffs • turnarounds • movable scales and soloing techniques • string bending • utilizing the entire fingerboard • and more. This second edition now includes audio and video access online!

00142420 Book/Online Media................................$19.99

FRETBOARD MASTERY
INCLUDES TAB

by Troy Stetina

Untangle the mysterious regions of the guitar fretboard and unlock your potential. *Fretboard Mastery* familiarizes you with all the shapes you need to know by applying them in real musical examples, thereby reinforcing and reaffirming your newfound knowledge. The result is a much higher level of comprehension and retention.

00695331 Book/Online Audio $19.99

FRETBOARD ROADMAPS – 2ND EDITION

ESSENTIAL GUITAR PATTERNS THAT ALL THE PROS KNOW AND USE

by Fred Sokolow

The updated edition of this bestseller features more songs, updated lessons, audio tracks! Learn to play lead and rhythm anywhere on the fretboard, in any key; play a variety of lead guitar styles; play chords and progressions anywhere on the fretboard; expand your chord vocabulary; and learn to think musically – the way the pros do.

00695941 Book/Online Audio $15.99

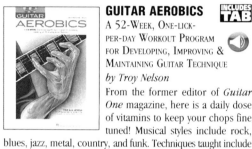

GUITAR AEROBICS
INCLUDES TAB

A 52-WEEK, ONE-LICK-PER-DAY WORKOUT PROGRAM FOR DEVELOPING, IMPROVING & MAINTAINING GUITAR TECHNIQUE

by Troy Nelson

From the former editor of *Guitar One* magazine, here is a daily dose of vitamins to keep your chops fine tuned! Musical styles include rock, blues, jazz, metal, country, and funk. Techniques taught include alternate picking, arpeggios, sweep picking, string skipping, legato, string bending, and rhythm guitar. These exercises will increase speed, and improve dexterity and pick- and fret-hand accuracy. The accompanying audio includes all 365 workout licks plus play-along grooves in every style at eight different metronome settings.

00695946 Book/Online Audio $19.99

GUITAR CLUES
INCLUDES TAB

OPERATION PENTATONIC

by Greg Koch

Join renowned guitar master Greg Koch as he clues you in to a wide variety of fun and valuable pentatonic scale applications. Whether you're new to improvising or have been doing it for a while, this book/audio pack will provide loads of delicious licks and tricks that you can use right away, from volume swells and chicken pickin' to intervallic and chordal ideas. The online audio includes 65 demo and play-along tracks.

00695827 Book/Online Audio $19.99

INTRODUCTION TO GUITAR TONE & EFFECTS

by David M. Brewster

This book/audio pack teaches the basics of guitar tones and effects, with online audio examples. Readers will learn about: overdrive, distortion and fuzz • using equalizers • modulation effects • reverb and delay • multi-effect processors • and more.

00695766 Book/Online Audio $16.99

PICTURE CHORD ENCYCLOPEDIA

This comprehensive guitar chord resource for all playing styles and levels features five voicings of 44 chord qualities for all twelve keys – 2,640 chords in all! For each, there is a clearly illustrated chord frame, as well as *an actual photo* of the chord being played! Includes info on basic fingering principles, open chords and barre chords, partial chords and broken-set forms, and more.

00695224..$19.95

SCALE CHORD RELATIONSHIPS
INCLUDES TAB

by Michael Mueller & Jeff Schroedl

This book teaches players how to determine which scales to play with which chords, so guitarists will never have to fear chord changes again! This book/audio pack explains how to: recognize keys • analyze chord progressions • use the modes • play over nondiatonic harmony • use harmonic and melodic minor scales • use symmetrical scales such as chromatic, whole-tone and diminished scales • incorporate exotic scales such as Hungarian major and Gypsy minor • and much more!

00695563 Book/Online Audio $14.99

SPEED MECHANICS FOR LEAD GUITAR
INCLUDES TAB

Take your playing to the stratosphere with the most advanced lead book by this proven heavy metal author. *Speed Mechanics* is the ultimate technique book for developing the kind of speed and precision in today's explosive playing styles. Learn the fastest ways to achieve speed and control, secrets to make your practice time really count, and how to open your ears and make your musical ideas more solid and tangible. Packed with over 200 vicious exercises including Troy's scorching version of "Flight of the Bumblebee." Music and examples demonstrated on the accompanying online audio.

00699323 Book/Online Audio $19.99

TOTAL ROCK GUITAR
INCLUDES TAB

A COMPLETE GUIDE TO LEARNING ROCK GUITAR

by Troy Stetina

This unique and comprehensive source for learning rock guitar is designed to develop both lead and rhythm playing. It covers: getting a tone that rocks • open chords, power chords and barre chords • riffs, scales and licks • string bending, strumming, palm muting, harmonics and alternate picking • all rock styles • and much more. The examples are in standard notation with chord grids and tab, and the audio includes full-band backing for all 22 songs.

00695246 Book/Online Audio $19.99

 **HAL•LEONARD**®

0319
032